To Jan C
(t.a.s.)

Friendship is a sheltering tree
A listening ear
A welcoming smile.

Friendship is a hug, a touch
Being there when times are sad,
Encouraging all along the way
Sharing laughter, fun, success.

Picking up where we left off
Our lifetime conversation.

Thank You

for all the

> *phrases*
> *ideas*
> *encouragement*
> *constructive criticism*
> *loving support*
> *walking alongside*

With special thanks to

Chris Rushton for permission to use a photograph of her painting

Clare Pollak and Ursula Dickenson for editorial assistance
Anne Constable for design advice

This is Not a Rehearsal

Maggie Simmonds

First published in 2012 by:
Red Priors Print
Lower End Cottage
CV47 7SP

ISBN: 978-0-9537084-1-3

Printed and bound in Great Britain by:
Proprint, Remus House, Coltsfoot Drive, Woodston,
Peterborough PE2 9BF

Contents

Life

Thoughts

Travels with Joy

Life

The Pink Garden Chair

It was love at first sight
When I saw it there,
Displayed on the floor
In a B&Q store:
A wonderful pink garden chair

We've had chairs galore of various hues,
Folding, recliners, browns, greens and blues.
Striped ones and floral ones, none ever so fair
As that beautiful pink garden chair.

I've a passion for pink as you can see,
Pink shoes, pink clothes, pink jewellery.
Having decided to grow old disgracefully
I'm thinking about pink hair
So **must have** matching pink garden chair.

It's in the sale, they'll soon be gone
And I've several pink-loving friends who'd really like one
But we've just been on holiday and our budget's on none.
While I know money doesn't come from thin air
I would dearly love a pink garden chair.

I set off round the shop to find what I needed
But try as I might, the vision never receded
And I found myself back for another wistful stare
At that magical pink garden chair.

A walk down the aisles as I seek a solution
Then, straight to the checkout with grim resolution
I will resist temptation!
Imagine then, the look of despair
When I arrived home with six pink garden chairs.

Well, actually

There was a little poetic licence there
In the saga of the lovely pink garden chair.
The truth is I only bought three
And just one of those was for me

Being Seen

Out walking in the country,
Not wearing my glasses,
I smile and speak to all I meet
In case someone who passes -
Not close enough to quite define their features -
Is one I know.
It would be so awful to ignore them.
We humans are such funny creatures,
When people start talking
Who knows what rumours might stem
From not speaking when out walking.

A Country Lad

My Dad was a country lad he walked several miles to school
And to chapel three times on a Sunday - that was his mother's
rule.
He enjoyed school and liked his teacher.
In those days things were so much stricter
And he once got the stick for not raising his hat to the vicar.
Holiday times he'd be out in the fields with all sorts of things in
his pockets
Doing odd jobs to earn a few bob like bull-walloping to 'Ucheter'
market.
In summer he'd collect wood for fires on winter evenings
When they'd make a rug of cloth pieces pegged into sacking.

One fine Sunday he went with his father to visit a distant aunt
On the way he saw a wheelwright's with barrows,
a float and a cart.
And he knew what he wanted to do - spend his life creating in
wood.
At last he was sixteen and could
Become an apprentice with official indentures.
He cut down trees as part of his training,
Learnt all the skills of jack, smooth and try planing
Graduating from primer to undercoat, top coat - and varnish,
finally
Building ladders and tyre shutting which was done at the smithy.
Learning his craft took five years, under the direction of his
mentor
Before he became a wheelwright, joiner and carpenter
And set up in business on his own.

When war broke out he was in no doubt, he'd go and serve his
nation.
He closed down his workshop and went to join up
Only to learn his was a reserved occupation.
So he spent the war travelling to jobs around the country
And when peace came he worked in a factory.

He settled down and lived in town but his heart wasn't there
He yearned for space and quiet and fresh, clear air.
Eventually, when I was three, he moved us back to the country
To a pump in the garden and no electricity
To a home in the heart of the sunset.
He made a workshop in a stable which meant he was able
To practise his skills at nights and weekends,
To repair the float a milkman asked him to mend,
Make dolls houses, cots, desks, stools and work boxes.
He did jobs for local farmers and was an accomplished gardener
Growing sweet peas and veg in his home on the country's edge.
A 'Country Bumpkin' to the last,
He departed this life at Candlemas.
His ashes are spread under a tree
In a crematorium where you can see
The rolling fields of his home county.
A view that would make him glad
That country lad, my Dad.

My Granny Was a Witch (they said!)

My Granny was a witch they said
She had steel grey hair in a coiled plait on her head
She was quite tall with a pointy nose
And often wore unusual clothes.
She was rather strict and could look very stern
You didn't ever dare to speak out of turn.

She used to go out late at night
When someone came to fetch her.
It would sometimes be quite far away
And then you'd hear the very next day
That a person who'd been ill was better.
So I think her witch variety was alright.

Well this is all rumour, isn't it?
We sat in the conservatory and she taught me to knit.

Blackberrying - Then And Now

A leisurely pursuit on long, lazy, late summer afternoons
With the sun mellowing, bees murmuring, birds gathering.
Warmed berries oozing juice staining hands, mouth and clothes
Time gently flows and, it seems, goes
On
Forever.

Those magic expeditions in childhood
Through fields, thickets and Henhurst wood
Where earlier in the year we'd found anemones.
Reaching up and over for the biggest luscious fruits
Scratched arms and legs despite the wellie boots
Home seemed so far away
Another world, another day.

Well I'm going this morning while it's still damp with dew
Before those clouds let go the rain they're forecast to
And I'll be wearing rubber gloves.
Hope the jam will taste as good.

Names

Why do we so seldom use our given names?
A girl at school was called Patricia
By her parents, that is, and the teachers
We all called her Pat.
Her friend was Christine,
Elegant-sounding, pristine,
But you only heard adults say that.

My parents gave me Margaret
And then wouldn't use it
As others might abuse it
And call me Maggie at school.
I think Maggie's quite cool.

A colleague Jacky's friends called her Jack
Her psychologist asked how she felt about that.
Bet, Jas and Lou, Jim, Bill and Ed,
Most names, it seems, get shortened.
If a one-syllable name is your good fortune
Someone's always tempted to add an 'i' or 'y' handle.
It seems so funny - the one we start with we rarely use.
Perhaps it's because, if we were our parents,
That's the one we just wouldn't choose?

Gardening Club

If you're keen on horticulture you could
Think about joining a gardening club.
There's something on offer all the time,
Outings, talks, cheese and wine,
Trips to members' gardens, Barnsdale and Wisley.
Fired with enthusiasm you return to work busily
Trying to emulate and adapt what you've seen:
Wet gardens, shade areas, borders 'hot', white or green.

The driving force, of course, is your committee
They work so hard you may feel guilty
About not making more of a contribution.
Members can play their part - bring a raffle prize for a start,
Grow plants to be sold for the kitty
And vote in line with the constitution.

You can join Boddington, Badby or clubs further afield
And enter competitions for the 'Best Gardener' shield.
If your dahlias or onions win a prize
You then set your sights and eyes
On achieving higher accolades next year.
You get discount on your seeds
Help with identification of weeds
And chance to make new friends who live near.

With all this input and inspiration
You're catapulted into creation
Striving all daylight hours
In sun, wind and showers
To achieve the perfect garden.
By the time you get to the meeting
All you can think about is sleeping
And may need to beg the presenter's pardon
For dozing off while they're speaking.

Empty Buildings

Barns, cow-sheds, hovels and homes
Centuries of country life these buildings have known.
Warm red brick and mellow local stone
They now stand empty.
Some solid and solitary crying out to be used
Others with sliding slates and gaping holes in bowing roofs.
Shepherds, dairy maids, labourers and farmers
Worked, sheltered, lived, loved and hid in these buildings'
corners.
They've disappeared gradually as materials have been taken
For new farm buildings, houses and ever more extensions.
Some of them are recognised as having "now" potential
Converted into modern homes or rural holiday rentals

Family Ties

A ram
Astride a ewe
On the brow of the hill.
Did the earth stand still?
Function complete
He returned to four feet
And stepped alongside,
Eye to eye.
A look passed between
How much did it mean?
Turning away
He left her to play the role of parent.

A lamb
Gangly and new
On the side of the hill
While its mother stands still
Sucks at her teat
Desperate to be replete
Then plays alongside.
If that ram walked by
This family scene
How much would it mean?

Would he recognise himself as parent?

Welcome Rain

Waking up to that constant, firm, soothing sound:
Rain.
Smelling the earth, seeing plants respond to moisture
Again.
After weeks of dry days and nights
With grass growing brown
Leaves coming down
And flowers struggling to thrive:

RAIN!

I Heard the Cuckoo This Morning

Although I'd been waiting for it
The sound surprised me.
It was the middle of the morning
Not in the early hours as the first call used to be.
Perhaps it has changed trees.
Maybe it's a new generation
Or there are fewer than there were.
The sound delighted me, quickened my heart
Reassured me that life's framework is secure
The changing of seasons is as it was.

I heard the cuckoo this morning

Yes, I Heard the Cuckoo This Morning

I heard the cuckoo this morning
That long-awaited sound of renewal
Confirming what the hedges' new growth
And the spring flowers have been saying in colour
Over the past few weeks.

Despite the presence of war and destruction
Nature's framework remains.
With some variation the seasons continue
And life still is.

Bending Over the Garden

Bending over the garden, deep in thought,
Preparing the bed for a new setting of peas,
The first having been eaten by slugs,
I became aware of the complex conversation above me.

A chaffinch holding forth on the apple bough,
Whole body moving with its message to the world,
Blackbird in a tree, unseen, known by its tuneful melody.
So many sounds, from all directions
Each singer in a different bush or tree
Moving round its territory.

Cacophony of sound and vibration: summer garden alive with life

Summer Morning Cycle

Today the sun is high although it's not yet half-past six.
Wet grass,
Cold shadow – fingers have a winter tingle.
Ahead of me a young fox stands and stares,
Turns, a mass of tail
And is gone.

Sheep lie beneath shapely oaks
Alive in their new green.

Startling velvets of sun-caressed pansies
Framed by garden walls of sleeping houses
Frail pink fragrance of dog rose hedgerows.

As I return heavy grey is overtaking the clear blue in the sky.
Those who sleep have missed the fine part of this day.

*

Rabbits dart, sheep call,

wings flap as I pass.

as I begin the descent
a grey-blue blanket is rising on the horizon,
trees silhouetted against the mellow peachy yellow of morning

summer fragrances encased between hedges
temporarily undisturbed by exhaust fumes,
clover, kedlock, buttercup, mingle with the grass

Morning Moment

The molten rising sun and fading full moon
Face each other across the hemisphere:
Shadow and form.
Moments of artistry and colour
No palette could create

Thank You for The Privilege   *to Pam Jones*

Thank you for the privilege of walking alongside you,
Thank you for the knowing of being there with you.
You saw a need, espoused a cause,
Challenged authorities, helped to change laws.

Support began with a telephone line
For isolated, terrified victims
Afraid to show any outward sign
Of the subjugation they lived in.

You counselled, lobbied, studied, persuaded,
Inspired others and together created
A listening post, refuge, haven from fears.
Always growing, responding, as over the years
Constantly breaking new ground,
You helped people turn their lives round.

You were strong, had compassion and determination.
The very occasional tears, of frustration,
Few were permitted to see.
Thank you for sharing with me.

Domestic Violence

At the agreed time
An ordinary woman opened the door.
What she was taking waited on the kitchen floor:
Two suitcases, a group of bulging plastic sacks and her one
Piece of furniture
A metal waste bin filled with items from her home.
Hurriedly loading them into the boot of an everyday car
With her two daughters clutching toys
And a pet in a cage in the back
We drove away.
As we turned the corner of their street
There was a huge joint sigh of relief.
They had escaped before he came back
To say he was sorry and abuse her again.

Photograph

I am the tell-tale angle of the mouth
Firmly closed in resentment
Imprisoning the rebellion
At this dressing-up in ill-fitting finery
For the photo
To be hung,
Shown,
Owned.

I am the thumb pressing the hand
Of the confused child
Drawn into the charade
Behind the façade
Of a 'happy-family' photo
Obeying the command to smile.

I am the eyes whose steady gaze
Stands out from the dark background
Of fear and distrust,
Brought here to be captured for ever
On film.
Those who look closely clearly see
The truth behind the camera's lie.

New Friendship   *words for Rita*

I've found a new treasure, something precious to explore,
A multi-faceted diamond, an island with many shores.
I'm unwrapping it gently, layer by layer
It arrived quite recently and is giving me huge pleasure.
It contains laughter and smiles, covers years and miles
Shares dreams, experiences, plans for things to do.
This magical gift is called getting to know you.

and Martin

A Good Listening To

Eyes speak with welcoming clarity
Full-face smile draws me near
Light, presence, warmth, humanity
All offer a 'good listening to' here.

Seat in Hope Cove

The sun is sparkling on the even waves
In the early evening.
Others share this seat and applaud the view.
They don't share the sadness of losing you.
They enjoy being here, the place you loved
They enjoy your seat.

I can almost hear you cheer
"What a good idea
A seat to share
Just like the chair
That heard all the fears, the joys and the tears
In the shop where I served for so many years."

And I know that a part of you hears and is here.

Village Fete

Months of planning, weeks of collecting
Days of baking, sorting, pricing
And watching the weather forecast.
When the day arrives at last
A motley collection of vehicles and trailers
Assembles on the green in the morning
Spilling out coconut shies, chairs and tables
The urn, straw bales, skittles and awning,
Setting the scene for the village fete,
Important date in the community calendar.
Cups and saucers, plates and spoons,
Will everything be ready for the afternoon?
Has everyone had a reminder?
Tradition demands an official 'Opener'
Ideally a brief, witty speaker
Well-known villager or maybe the vicar
To declare the event well and truly open.
People want to spend so speechmaking's a token.

Homemade cakes on the WI stall,
First port of call, a free for all.
Elbows allowed, manners do have their limits,
It's always the same, cakes sold out in minutes.
The bottle stall is a big attraction
Everyone looking for the satisfaction
Of a nought or five ending which means they've a winner.
Plants, flowers, fruit, preserves, it's all
Home-grown on the produce stall.
How many eggs will this hen lay?
Is the island's treasure in its hills or bay?
How many sweets does this jar hold?
Guess the name of the doll or maybe a teddy.

By then you're quite sure to be ready
To stop and enjoy some refreshment.
Better sit down before it's too late.
Cakes on dainty china plates
Scones with cream, victoria sponges
Shortbread, flapjack, chocolate munchies.
Tea from an ancient mammoth teapot,
Make sure you go when they've mashed a new lot
Freshly-brewed, not stewed.
Sometimes there's a band or piano accordion
And games for youngsters to take part in,
Wheelbarrow, sack or egg and spoon races,
Fancy dress and painted faces.
The bric-a-brac tables are piled high.
At the end of the day there'll be a huge sigh
From the organiser of the stall
'What will we do with it all?
Although we've made a lot of sales,
I'm afraid we've totally failed
To get rid of everybody's 'unwanteds',
It looks not much less than when we started'.

By half-past four the refreshments have gone
Coconuts knocked down, prizes won
The raffle's been drawn,
The doll's named - it's Dawn.
Plenty of books still and lots of apples
The money is yet to be counted
Will the takings be more or less than before?
Whatever the result everyone is quite sure
That all their efforts amounted to
A good village 'do'

The Badminton Hut, water colour by Chris Rushton

The Badminton Hut

The Badminton Hut was the place to be.
It doubled up as playgroup and surgery
Transformed by night with cabarets, cartwheels
And cancans exposing hips to heels.
The wooden floor was good for dancing
Sometimes a bit gritty for yoga when toddlers had been prancing
Around tipping up the sand tray.
Was it a Wednesday or a Monday
When a lorry drove through the wall
And divided in half the hall?
There is a story, tho' it may be a fable
That a certain couple met there – under a table

Now the WI, the jumbles and gardening club sales
The weddings and parties and rural markets
Have all moved over the road.
The hut's plot's been built on,
The village hall's a new one.
With smart kitchen and showers
It extends to two storeys.
It's the base for the Fun Run
When hundreds come
And some people do still play badminton

Monday Morning Ballet Class

The pre-school ballet pupils
In their fairy wings and tutus
And their tiny, dainty ballet shoes,
Are going home with Mum.

Who's this now arriving,
Walking, cycling and driving?
It's the Monday ladies ballet class.
We've got no exams to pass
We are here for fun.

It's a mix of shapes and ages
A few did ballet to various stages
Most of us are complete beginners
And hope the exercise will make us thinner.

Warm up first so we don't do any harm
Par de bourré and rond de jambe
Pliés and glissés show how fit we are
As we do our work-out at the windowsill barre.

We follow our teacher, Miss Lorraine:
Our movements are never quite the same
As her graceful, balanced ones.

Time for floor work, this should flatten the stomach
And the next exercise is a challenging sit-up.
Just do your best if you aren't double-jointed.
Lift and stretch, keep that toe pointed,

Into the centre for the routine we're learning,
I wish I could remember the steps.
It has little jumps and complicated turnings
And we haven't perfected it yet.

We didn't start at three
So we're never going to be
At Saddlers Wells or featured on TV
For us it's about feeling free.

For this magical forty-five minutes
Our expression knows no limits
As we move to ballet music's evocative sound
With smiles of encouragement all around
We live our childhood dream.

Career Choices

While he works and lives away
We can meet up for a day
Enjoy a meal, see a play.
I can look at him and say
"It's good to be with you"

Other mothers must live in fear
Dreading news they never want to hear
About sons and daughters equally dear
Whose work means danger is always near.
Will they return home safely?

With each grim bulletin we see
Reporting another life ceased to be
Sad for those families, I reflect thankfully,
My relief that our son chose to be
A teacher not a soldier.

Changing Stiles   (Or Styles Of Stiles)

'Twas on a Monday morning the footpath officer came to call.
He looked at the field gate and said 'This won't do at all.
It's tied up with string and it doesn't have a hinge
This sort of thing makes the ramblers whinge'

"That wasn't the reason we called you.
We're concerned about our stile,
The sleeper across the ditch has been dodgy for a while.
It's rotting and has holes which look dangerous
And we wouldn't want anyone to sue the council - or us"

It was a Wednesday morning when the workforce arrived
Sporting green footpath department sweaters with apparent pride.
They dug out the heavy clay, luckily it wasn't wet
And concreted in a round metal post which they then left to set.
So it was actually on Thursday that we saw the transformation
Combined pedestrian and field gate in perfect integration.

On Friday it was the turn of our stile:
Only one worker so it took quite a while
To remove the heavy sleeper
And make good the area around the new innovation -
Which was quite a revelation -
A two-thirds circle of metal enclosing a gate which practically
Closes automatically.

Yes, our stile's gone romantic,
It's become a kissing-gate
No more clambouring antics,
Much easier to negotiate.
So now we're completely modern
With much better access
But you know, I must confess,
I liked our wooden stile.

Village Harvest

The church bells summon as they have, it seems, for ever
Calling the people of Hardwick together
To celebrate and give thanks for earth's abundance.
Those walking to church may think and talk
Of our ancestors who came on foot or horse.
Now it's cars and four by fours.

The harvest's in, it's been a good year
The contractors managed to complete around here
Without wind and rain to spoil the crops.
It's plough, harrow and sow once harvesting stops,
The wheel of the year continues apace.

Gardens have given us fruit, flowers and veg.
Plus wild nuts and berries from the hedge
Foods to eat now, preserve or freeze
On cold winter days the taste buds to please.

Once the whole village took part in harvesting
Before 'do-it-all' machinery the sheaves needed stooking.
Tea was brought out to the fields in baskets
On days which glow golden and warm in the memory.
The church overflowed with harvest gifts,
Rows of apples adorned the pews,
Sheaf-shaped loaves baked for the occasion,
Children brought filled boxes as their contribution
Everyone wore their Sunday best, worshipped together,
Shared the news.

While relatively few people now till the land
As most villagers' employment is compute or commute,
Many are prepared to lend a hand
In the village regularly, doing their bit quietly:

Cutting the grass, winding the clock
Ensuring there's communion wine in stock.
Banking the money, maintaining the books
Keeping an eye on how the churchyard looks.
Making sure the floodlights are working.
Chairing meetings, checking the heating,
In the local school listening to children reading.

Individuals may spend hours
Adorning the church with art work and flowers
Visiting neighbours who feel alone
Or simply being at the end of a phone.
Youth group leaders encourage their members
To live life fully while considering others,
The same young people who sing carols for charity
And look after pets when their owners go on holiday.

There are now few occasions in the year
When a large congregation gathers here.
This is one event to which people will come,
To raise that song of Harvest Home
And meet together afterwards for the traditional supper.
Missing some familiar faces,
Welcoming new ones to those places
Thankful that it's peaceful here,
For plentiful food, clean water and air.
The cycle of life goes on.

October Afternoon

We walk along together
A couple of yards apart
Crossing the slope in the October sun
You pushing the mower, me the barrow
You cutting grass, me harvesting leaves.
They will make compost and leafmould
To bloom our flowers and feed our veg
Which will in turn feed us
As we walk along together.

Beachy Head

The pub is packed with half-term-outing families
Eating lunch.
Children of all ages scramble in the wind
On the grassy heights.
Yellow white cliffs shine in the sun.

You wouldn't do it on a sunny day, would you?
Sunshine always says there's hope,
Good things ahead -
Life, love, companionship.

The Samaritans' phone number,
And the stone which quotes the psalmist
Remind us that in the dark night of the soul
There may be no light.

If someone you knew died here
You'd need to come
And stand
And look
And wonder
And ask 'Why?'
Wouldn't you?

The sun disappears and cloud shadows make monsters on the sea.

Alternative November

Finished-with stubble on set-aside land
Frames a field of winter wheat,
Brilliant green, three inches high.
The sky is high, bright, light,
Horizon clouds tinged purple
By the full, round, magnetic yellow-white morning sun.
Bathed in its light shining, scarlet-shining rose-hips
Offer themselves to birds and vitamin-full jams
To ward off winter's ills.
A bow-legged Guy-Fawkes-scarecrow rescued from a bonfire
Standing sentry on the field reminds:
Yes, it is November

Yellow-Gold

The yellow-gold of autumn
Lies on the ground,
Its brilliance reflecting
To the grey November sky.
Surrendering to the rake
It is piled to rot
And later renew the garden:
The trees it clothed shapely beautiful
In their nakedness

Middle One

'You're my Middle One'
after the first born
for a while her baby
and some years her youngest
till a third arrived completing the family.
'My Middle One'
a title bestowed with so much love
I wore it like a crown.

Special   *for Clare*

I wanted to be special,
To be told I was,
To know I really mattered
And would be
A wonderful being.
Not famous, not brilliant,
Just special.

Today you told me I am.

Redundant

Lines
Of words
On a page
Confirm what I have been told.
I am redundant.
'We regret'
And I know they do.
'There isn't the money' – and that's true too.
Whatever the reason,
However nicely it's said,
The fact remains:
I have no choice.

Someone Who Knows the World
- in praise of Wendy Cope

She's got it that woman,
She knows where it's at.
She can say things succinctly
In four lines flat
Or in verse which is longer
And takes time to spin
The web of a story which entices us in.
She knows all the theory and technicalities
Of rhythm and syntax and iambic pentameters.
She's learned and well-read, her books are bestsellers.
She can be funny or serious and she has the measure of fellas.
When it comes to writing poems
She can really do the biz.
She's got it that woman,
She tells it like it is.

Ending

That's it, it's over.
The last form signed
And final words exchanged.
No more contact required,
No need to meet again.
The only thing left to do
Is to change the name.

Poetry Group

We come with our books at which we've had a good look -
If we haven't been too busy.
If that's not been the case and the day's been a race
We may simply choose something easy.

We relax in comfortable seats
The host's usually first to read
Then each one follows in turn
Varying our voices while sharing our choices,
From traditional and current we learn.
It's always a feast
From the longest to the least
Each verse has something cogent to say.
A few we don't quite comprehend -
Sometimes it's that line at the end
Which lifts the veil away.

When they depict the season there's an obvious reason
Why some choices reflect each other.
With others, though we haven't conferred
A synergy will emerge
As though when we prepare there's something in the air
Linking thoughts and feelings -
Making the evenings
Perfect symphony.

You Never Really Get Used to It

When they first arrive, there's no escape
You're stuck to each other like sellotape.
You feed, clothe and comfort all the time
Try to banish the colic with a nursery rhyme.

After a while you realise you can
Safely leave them with a friend or their Gran
Or even a babysitter.

Then it's playgroup and nursery and you get to know
That they can be sociable and you can let go.
That first day at school, you say 'Goodbye'
And walk away with a tear in your eye
A lump in your throat and the desperate hope
That they, you and the teacher can cope.

As they progress through the system there's less need for Mum
You're there in the background and may feel a bit glum.
"Now let's be positive, it's more time for me
To do what I'd like till they come home for tea".
Truth is, you're probably juggling work with school runs
Which have to be negotiated with the other Mums.

And then appears a new responsibility -
Learning to live with a teenage personality.
Was this being ever my baby?
Sleepless nights reappear.
You wonder where and how they are
And whether they and their friends are safe in your car.

Next it's work or college and maybe travels abroad.
No point in worrying tho' you scan the billboards
For news of air crashes, a coup or hurricane
And are delighted and relieved to see them home again.

Eventually it happens, they get their own place, be it flat, canal
boat or house
And one day you realise that that 'new face' has become a partner
or spouse.
You take pride in your offspring, admire things they do
And quietly think in some ways they're like you.

You may find new roles as Grannie and Gramps
And whenever you're asked, you jump at the chance
To be with the grandchildren: all those stories to be told.
Your child is maturing, their life is unfurling
And you realise you're growing old.

However frequently you see them
Farewells always bring a sigh
You never really get used to saying "Goodbye"

Reminiscing

We were a single lingering kiss on an African dance floor
As I was too unsure to follow you into the Sub-Saharan night.
I saw you once back here at the theatre
In animated conversation with a woman.
I didn't approach.
Sitting here at a pre-performance talk
In your home town, I wonder;
Will our children ever meet?
Did your rich black hair become 'distinguished grey'?

I don't remember your name

Canal Shopping

If you find yourself without a car
Relocate to Leamington Spa.
As long as you've something that stays afloat
And an oar to steer, you can go by boat.
Sainsbury, Asda and Tesco are all
Easily accessible from the canal.

The Farmer's Footprint

He wanders purposefully across the field
Walking meditation
Hands clasped behind his back, a slight figure.
The sun glints on his glasses
As he turns to look at each sheep.
He knows every animal, every corner, each foot print.

He feels this land, he lives this land.
"Yes, the grass has taken well"
The sheep are clearly thriving on it.
"I'm not planting corn any more and I won't be lambing again"
He'll buy ewe lambs for growing on:
"Don't know how much money that will make,
 It's a way of life"
Not just a job, a calling, a business or a career.
A way of life.
And he's adapting this 'way of life' living
To his advancing years.

Summer Morning Realisation

Sunlight radiance on this field
Enticed me away from my usual route
Arresting the attention of my senses -
Hedges, trees and grass exuding new green,
Bathed in brightness.

Alone in the centre of this verdant newness
Lay a dull-dead ewe,
Rounded by motherhood
Yet life-less.

This juxtaposition shocked, intruded on the day's joy
And then unlocked the realisation
That to go in a season of creation,
Departing on a wave of new life,
Is a natural transition desirable to the human condition.

This is how I could choose to go –
No winter languishing in urine-odoured residential corridors.
"For what is it to die but to stand naked in the wind
And melt into the sun?"*

* from 'On Death', Khalil Gibran

Abandoned Roses

Red roses.
Lovers' roses?
Lying on the path on a Malvern hill,
Half of them still in cellophane,
Half lying strewn on the ground.

They don't have the appearance of tribute
Or acknowledgement of a death,
Not laid carefully or lovingly enough.
Did someone bring them to give to a living loved one?
Was it a proposal refused or a quarrel not made up,
No bridges built or forgiveness offered?
They are darkest red still, despite the dust
And lie here beautiful,
Abandoned.

Village Farewell to Nell

Shire village sunshine
Gently caresses the loving group
Assembled for the farewell
To celebrate her being.
The hillside ancient church
Full to its altar
Powerful living testament
To her fruitful life and service.

Groups and individuals whose lives she touched
Giving, listening to, doing for and being with,
Each with their own smile of memory,
Richer having known her, saddened by her passing,
Together raising sound of song.

Powerfully poignant poem
Spoken in loving courage and hopefulness.
Words of condolence,
Silent contemplation.

Short walk to a green resting place
Between Bredon and the Malverns.
Rose petals sprinkled with the earth
Bring her living garden to her grave.

Thoughts

Alive

Glory of a frostbright early morning
Combining with our own spring-awakening
Bird song, dew-bedecked grass
Buds swelling
Nature
Telling

Thoughts

The clouds are light
The morning moon is bright
The day will unfold
And return to night
Followed by tomorrow

*

The darkness is now
Just two small windows
And even in that darkness
There are stars.

*

It's now
I'm me
I'm free
To be.

Removing the dying Sumach tree
Made space for the sun flowers

*

It is sometimes in the
Most exquisite
That we feel our deepest pain.

*

You offer me three wishes
I ask only two:
Life-energy
And the mantle of peace

*

Love is a state of being

Life

"Well what's it all about then?"
"There's all this
  Junk
  That's
  Dumped
  Over
  The
  Years
  And we have to let it go."

Snowbow

Rising sun behind,
Dark blue clouds in front
A perfect semi-circle of the seven colours
Tips horizon to horizon.
The only moisture in the air
White flakes of winter.
Can this be a Snowbow?

Silver Lining

While I don't like wind,
Until it blew
I didn't notice you
High-growing full-blown rose.

Unseasonal

Slightly wizened,
Coloured the deepened yellow of autumn sun,
Last fruits hang on the japonica
Their branch companions
New season red-tipped tiny leaves
Protecting flowers in miniature
Whose mature scarlet
Decorated
Pre-climate-change Maypoles.

It is mid-January.

Inevitability

The single chestnut in the boundary wood
Clutches her fruit in tight, spiked hold
Taunting would-be gatherers
Until, unable to resist nature and the inevitable
She surrenders to the bursting open
And flaunts her bounty

Impressions   *of a private viewing*

Feed the Horses: life is basic
Love Song: raw red
            cool blue
            timid green,
            white hot music.
The inevitable heart.
Blood drops into the grey surrounding stream
Of non-love.
And I wanted to hear you say sing the **Poem Song**
Aloud.
Swirls and straight lines of **Notation 1**
Colour and contrast
Boats on the water
Grass in rainbow swamp
Or nothing at all of this?
And **Notation 2**? Yes, just less exciting.
'**Yes**' yummy colour.
Drawn miles onto that central butterfly shape
And thrown onto the oceans below, **MMM2**
Intrigues
Fascinates
Captures
And leaves me
Transported.
Listen Hum Quantum Hum
Is deep when approached a second time,
So different from the side.
Another world.
Contrasts of lines and parasols and delicious colours.
Overtones expressing the depths and twists
And tongue contortions,
The cavities and ravines
Dropped into when creating.

Travels with Joy

Windy Ride

My challenge for today
Is to cycle in the wind.
It's wild, it's rough.
Will I have enough
Energy
To get anywhere at all?

It's creating a vacuum
I cycle in slow motion
Against an invisible wall.

And then the lull.
I'm freed
To cycle at speed.

I flew with the wind
I laughed at the wind.
It buffeted and teased me,
And yes, it even pleased me
To play at this game with the wind.

I cycled in the wind
It was rough and it was tough
And I did have enough
Energy
To go there and return.

Chapel of St Julitte, Tintagel

"Dad, what's this?"
"You're standing in the chapel,
It was built a thousand years ago."
"What's that?"
"It's the altar
Where the priest would be
When people met here to worship."
"What's worship?"
"It's when you pray."

The mist closes in,
The wind blows around this half-ruined space
And the atmosphere created
In four hundred years of praise
Is tangible
Today.

The Great Carnation Robbery

Leaving the restaurant she paused at each table
To smell the single carnation.
Standing side-ways to the bar he was able
To observe her and she caught his imagination.
Swiftly crossing the room
He plucked a bloom
And followed her towards the door
Where she turned and saw
His daring.
In a conspiratorial moment of sharing
He handed her the flower.
A spark ignited.
She thanked him, delighted,

And went to catch the boat

Toad in the Road

We found a toad
In the road
Sitting upright, it seemed alert.
It didn't move as we approached,
Just sat in the road.

Concerned
We touched it, softly.
It fell over, cold. Dead?
Gently we put it on the roadside
Hoping it would revive

And cycled on.

Claydon Top Lock

Just up from boring number eighteen?
Claydon Top Locks is a very different scene.
Welcoming building surrounded by flowers
Pose here for a picture of happy hours.
Forget how you 'nearly died'
Working the 'Napton Flight'
When the sun was at its height
And you couldn't think why you'd ever thought that
Two weeks on a canal boat
Would feel like a holiday.
When you look at this photo you'll say
"Yes, we'd love to do it again, the opposite way"

One day …

Wintry Langley Dam

Green clarity
Cold, calm, clear landscape,
Nature's essence perfectly reflected.
Depths of water, thought and being
Beckoning to heights previously unknown.
Human detail fishing boat.

Wind Turbines

We sat on a flat stone hidden by rushes
Looking across the Cemmaes valley
A green palette of grass, ferns and mosses,
Misty mountains to the west.
On the opposite skyline
A cluster of wind turbines
Slowly turning, a gentle mesmerising movement
Flowing anticlockwise with their own simplicity
Blending with the ancient ridge
An incongruous bridge across time.

Helvellyn on a Fine Day
for Tom - who wouldn't choose the easy route

If the Youth hostel is where you stay
You're already on the way.
No toiling up from Glenridding.
Passing the places where lead was mined
This path was part of the daily grind,
Miners walked it to work every day.
Over a gated wooden bridge you wander
In a pleasant meander
Slowly getting higher going round to go up
Switch-back pattern
Skirting the water.
Then it starts getting tougher.
The peak's in sight,
It looks quite a height
And there's rough terrain to be covered
Before gaining it.

Stones and boulders now, the path's disappeared
No clear way here
As you look down on Red Tarn
While scrambling up Striding Edge.
Sheer drop that side, try to the right.
Wouldn't want to attempt this
In mist or at night.
At the end of the ridge
Look back where you've come
Snaking your way towards the summit.
Feel pleased you've done it.

The next bit's quite easy compared to the last
And when you get to the top
There's a stone sheltering spot
Where you can sit and enjoy some repast
Alongside the rest of the current cohort.

The prop forward clad in Gilberts shorts,
Exhausted by the climb
Greets everyone there
Then takes his time
To enjoy his chicken pie.
The 'professional' couple 'warming up for the day'
From Settle to Penrith are on their way.
Individuals keeping themselves to themselves
Eat sandwiches from home or supermarket shelves.
Views to the Solway and is that Morecombe Bay?

Setting off down via
The less challenging route
Surrounded by circles of ribbons of peaks
With an outer ridge of never-ending summits,
The path winds up and down and over
Created by humans and sheep.
White-headed brown sheep
White-spotted black sheep
From hamlets tree-speckled below.

Look from Bassenthwaite across to Ullswater
And there's Skiddaw, in the middle.
We'll leave that for tomorrow.

Cycling in Yorkshire

In every town you may come down
To enter it
But oh, the ups to leave it.
A hill ahead, low gear or walk.
It seems to end at the bend.
When you get there, some despair
To see it goes on rising.
Climb up that bit, keep on, chin up,
Then surely comes the summit.
Alas, it's not, there's more to climb,
The bike feels heavier all the time
And the hill goes on and on.

This pattern repeats itself time and again,
You feel exhausted and just when
You think you can't go on,
It really is the final part
Negotiate this and you can start
To free wheel,
Flying down at speed
Feeling free:
Until you see
The next hill up ahead...

Motorway Ben Nevis

We're off to Fort William
We're climbing the Ben
Will it be lonely, even dangerous,
Will we get down again?

The path is a steep one.
We meet others descending
As we make our way up.
"Have you been to the top?"
"Ja, natürlich", "Mais oui" "Sure have".

We clambered
And sweated
Our way towards the top.
Other people had the same idea
There were hundreds!
Well, quite a lot.
A blister on the heel
Both legs feel
Achey.
Those coming down smiled
And encouraged us on, while
The views
Came and went
As we walked through clouds
To the sun.
The top!
No, it's not,
Just a marker on the way.
"Ten more minutes, easy walking",
I heard one man say.
     We will
         Make it now

Yes, that's it, that's the top
All those people
       And stones

What's that, like a building,
Near the refuge for storms?
Surely no-one could live here
In this barren place?
We must make some enquiries
When we get back to base

We made it, we've done it,
We climbed up the Ben.
Not quite the first –
Count the number here, ten
Twenty, thirty, forty,
There's really quite a crowd
Of adults and children.
Still we can be proud
We all reached the top.

So back down we go
We'll do this without strain.
Well maybe not, it seems
This stony terrain
Is as tough going down
As it was coming up.

Back at the bottom
We see an exhibition
On the path's history
In the 19th century.

One man walked up here
Every day for two years
To check on the weather
And gather information,
With a pony and dog
His only companions.

The ruin we saw
Right up at the top
Was once a hotel
For travellers to stop.
Adventurous Victorians
On pony or foot
Made an overnight stay
And came down the next day.

We're leaving Fort William
We're now moving on,
The Cairngorms the next stop,
More mountains to climb.
Ben Nevis was busy our photos will show.
Shall we come back in winter?
Might be quieter in snow!

The Standing Stones of Callanish

Smooth grey lines with gentle bend
As if braced against the Hebridean wind.
For centuries half lost beneath
The layered peat of Callanish.
Now fully visible again
Their slender greyness greets the sun
When it shines between the clouds.
Americans and Antipodeans come
To stand in awe and wonder why
This place of peace was formed.
Cereal farmers tilled the land
Five thousand years ago
And later generations burned
Their dead protected by
These Standing Stones of Callanish.
Hooded figure, dreaming youth,
Wizened elder, dour chief,
Pale shades of pink and green and mauve,
Mingled with the grey:
Who here now can say
What time-held secrets lie beneath
The Standing Stones of Callanish?

Harris

Rounded hills
White-topped by stone
Treeless
Bare.
Grey-clouded sky
Peat deep slopes
Which sheep alone
Inhabit
And there are water-lilies flowering in the loch.

Left Behind

So many empty, falling-down,
Abandoned houses,
Piles of stone.
Remains of Black Houses
Some roofless, otherwise intact,
Often alongside newer, inhabited homes
Of people of these islands now.
Why do they leave these relics of the past?
Is it the cost of pulling them down,
The difficulty of moving the stone away,
Or is it, perhaps, the promises made
To those who left for distant shores
Hoping to return some day?

Orkney Tak

Tak, gentle Orkney,
Blue rolling folding hills,
Pyramid stooks
Wholesome inquisitive cattle,
Expansive infinite skies.
Wildflower weeds portrait-like
Indelible, indestructible peace.
Soft-spoken gentleness,
Light-breezed peace.
Tak, Orkney, tak

Travels on a Honda   *- many seasons ago*

'2010, 2010, where are you going to, 2010?'
'The market for vegetables and bread
Warm groundnuts in a paper cone
And mouth watering mangoes. If they're not in season
Maybe I'll find guavas instead'.
'O'bruni, o'bruni'
'Dasiba'.* 'Naa'. 'Dasiba'. 'Naa'.

'2010, 2010, where are you going to, 2010?'
'Govco the college where I'm working
And the student teachers are training
They're preparing lesson notes and making visual aids.
Soon they'll be doing some teaching
At Bagabaga Primary and Gumbihini Middle schools
Practising what they've been learning
'O'bruni, o'bruni'
'Dasiba'. 'Naa'. 'Dasiba'. 'Naa'.

'2010, 2010, where are you going to, 2010?'
'The dressmaker with this cloth from the market
She'll make me a traditional outfit
With a fitted top and wraparound skirt
Good for riding on Mammy lorries to keep out dust and dirt.'
'O'bruni, o'bruni'
'Dasiba'. 'Naa'. 'Dasiba'. 'Naa'.

'2010, 2010, where are you going to, 2010?'
'Back to my home on Education Ridge
For a shower with a bucket and cold drink from the fridge
Then I'll sit on the steps in the shade of the Nim tree
And listen to its fruits dropping down all around me'.
'O'bruni, o'bruni'
'Aninwula*' 'Naa'

*'Dasiba' is Good Morning, 'Aninwula', Good Evening in Dagbani.
'Naa' is the response. 2010 was the scooter's registration number

Harmattan

Dusty, breezy, dry and hot
Hot   hot   hot.
Sunlight and clarity disappear.
Overcast, yet no rain falls from the heavy, loaded sky.
Wind roughening, howling,
Whipping up dust till the air is thick.
Eating dust through the brown-red haze of sunset.
Waiting for the cool of morning

Frangipani

The African day slips into dark.
Intense heat soothes into balm.
Frangipani flowers resplendent in daylight
Perfume and inspire the night

Sight of The Condor

'Don't avalanche yourselves," our guide had cautioned
As we prepared ourselves for this adventure.
He spoke of altitude effects and pristine nature,
Environmental respect, the need for water,
And *possible* sighting of the legendary condor, seen only at
height.

No thought of speed now,
Walking at a creep
Along a steep and ancient Inca trail.
Slowly, so slowly, foot by foot
Willing the breath-short body forward
In this clear-aired grandeur with icing-sugar Andean peaks.
Gradually we covered the distance, tempering the body's
resistance.

As we gained the Ankascocha Pass,
Height of experience, zenith of achievement,
Way above in the vast expanse of sky,
Hardly visible in the camera's eye,
Symbol of good fortune, deity and history,
A condor flew overhead.

Willowdene Welcome

The smiles of welcome are
As broad and warm
As the full Australian sun.
The open door,
Infectious laugh
Like the kookaburra on the fence
Project a sense
Of oneness, ease.

Free settlers all
Pioneers, engineers,
Men of the cloth
And farmers now,
Living and loving the land.
Caring, sharing whatever there is,
Cultivating and conserving,
Planting, gathering and preserving.
Hard work and courage
Good years and lean,
Boon times and drought's ravage
This family has seen.

It's all there now
Encompassed in
That warm and open welcome.

Listen to the Cry of the Earth

– reflections on a didgeridoo performance

The resonating floor holds

That primordial sound.

It frightens a part of me

While relaxing my being.

It haunts and delights me,

Permeates me with peace.

So strange

Yet familiar

Conjuring limitless landscapes

Once known long ago.

The Cry tears at my senses and fascinates my soul.

As soon as it ends

I yearn its return.

Travelling Companions   *to Michael*

We fix a date.
You smile quietly and prepare
Calculating distances, planning routes,
Checking the weather forecast.
When we walk you read maps and compass
When we cycle you check tyres and road signs.
I walk and ride alongside you, free to enjoy.
Thank you.

Hoar frost on winter trees
Fragrance and form of Lily-of-the-Valley in a May garden
Being held close in friendship
Finding your own adventures
Maturing with loved ones...
Enjoy life
This is not a rehearsal.